LETTER FROM THE EDITOR

Ten years. It goes by in the blink of an eye. As cliche as that may be, it is the truth. Here we are ten years later publishing the 10-year anniversary issue of Kandy Magazine. On August 31st, 2011, we published the first issue of KANDY Magazine featuring Tiffany Selby on the cover. Ten years later, we are honored to showcase Laurie Young on her 8th Kandy cover.

The Kandy connection between Tiffany and Laurie pre-dates our origins. Let's call it, The Story Behind the Story. You know, like that scene in Swingers when the cocktail waitress says to Vince Vaugh, or is it Jon Favreau, "Cocktails? The guy behind the guy."

"The Story Behind the Story" is before Kandy I owned a previous magazine. I had previously published Tiffany and Laurie in that magazine. Coincidentally, we photographed Tiffany and Laurie on the same day, in the same location.

Here we are, Laurie Young on the cover of our 10 Year Anniversary issue, ten years from when Tiffany Selby appeared on our very first cover.

Now, for a little background on the cover photo. Do you recall the commercial limerick, "What would you do for a Klondike bar?" In our own iteration, we inquire, "what would you do for a Kandy magazine cover?" In the case of Laurie Young, she agreed to pose to recreate what we feel is one of the more iconic video music moments. Little did Laurie realize that when she agree to recreate that iconic moment, it would require nearly an hour of standing under the spray of a garden hose and a day that would entail 1,800 photos. But, that is what it took to capture the cover shot as well as the accompanying interior pictorial.

So, to Laurie and Tiffany, and all the models who have appeared in Kandy in our first ten years, I raise a glass in your honor and say… Salud!

Cheers!

[signature]

Editor in Chief
Ron Kuchler

Editor-at-Large
Mike Prado

Managing Editor
David Packo

Associate Editor
Steve Scala

Director of Marketing
Bill Nychay

Cover Photo Credits
Photographer Mario Barberio
Hair and Makeup Liz Carrillo
Location Kandy Beach House

Contributors
Teddy Field, Mike Prado, Aaron Riveroll

Contact Us
Kandy Enterprises LLC
7260 W Azure Dr. Ste 140-639
Las Vegas, NV 89130
www.kandymag.com
facebook @kandymag
instagram @kandymagazine

General Inquiries - support@kandymag.com
Letters to The Editor - letters@kandymag.com
Copyright - legal@kandymag.com
Subscription Inquiries - subscriptions@kandymag.com

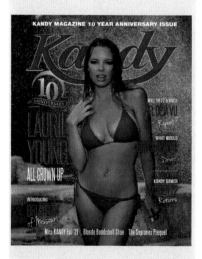

WHEELS
What Would Bruce Wayne Drive After a Breakup?
By Teddy Field

Well shit. You thought she was the one. But instead, she broke your heart. Or maybe you broke her heart. Either way, you're single, and the field is yours to play. But what do you drive? The answer depends on how much money you have...

Option A: You're Bruce Wayne Rich

2021 Mercedes AMG GT C Roadster
(pictured 2021 Mercedes-AMG GT Stealth Edition)
Starting Price: $165,000

Alright, so you just broke it off with Miss Connecticut, and it's time to announce to the A-List world that you are available. So, what do you drive? How about the 2021 Mercedes AMG GT C Roadster?

In reality, the 2021 Mercedes AMG GT C Roadster is really the third generation of the legendary Mercedes 300 SL roadster from the 1950s (the Mercedes SLS Roadster would have been the 2nd-Gen). Think of it as a Dodge Viper with a trust fund. Under that long hood is a front-mid-mounted twin-turbo 4.0L AMG V8 that dumps 523 hp onto the rear wheels with a truly violent soundtrack that's accentuated with off-throttle crackles and bangs. This car sounds so good, you won't ever want to turn on the stereo. Oh, it will also accelerate to 60 mph in just 3.6 seconds. This elegant-looking Mercedes is every bit a supercar but without the vulgarity of scissor doors and giant rear wings.

The 2021 Mercedes AMG GT C Roadster is an upgrade from the standard AMG GT Roadster with several really cool features like rear-wheel steering and a dry-sump oiling system for the engine. So, you can fling it into a corner, pulling some serious Gs, and the engine/turbos will still be lubricated by the pressurized oiling system. This car is a seriously advanced way to show off, and the styling will help you attract more ladies. Not 'hoes' looking to get famous on social media.

[Editor's Note: I'm Batman, damnit! As we were assembling imagery to accompany Teddy's masterpiece, we stumbled across the Stealth model. This new special edition includes the AMG Exterior Night Package, black brake calipers, the AMG radiator grille in dark chrome, headlamps with black elements, and mixed-size tires with 19-inch matte black Y-spoke wheels on the front, and 20-inch wheels on the rear. Other features of the "Stealth Edition" include the carbon-fiber roof with dark- tinted areas on the Coupe, and a black soft top on the Roadster. The interior of the "Stealth Edition" features the AMG Interior Night Package, AMG steering wheel in DINAMICA microfiber with black steering wheel spokes and shift paddles, upholstery in Exclusive nappa STYLE leather in black with diamond quilting, black topstitching and trim elements in black piano lacquer (optionally in carbon fiber/black piano lacquer). Simply put, it's your very own MINI Batmobile.]

Option B: You're Not Bruce Wayne Rich

2022 Toyota GR 86
Starting price: $29,000

Okay, it turns out she's not the love of your life. And you're not Thomas Wayne's only son, so you gonna have to pinch a few pennies to buy your next ride. Now stop sulking, sell that engagement ring and take the "wedding fund" down to your local Toyota dealer and get this: the 2022 Toyota GR 86. This RWD's sports car is basically like a Miata, but with rear seats and a fixed roof. It's also a lot more manly than a dinky little Mazda, so you're going to get a lot more attention from the fairer sex.

Like the previous Toyota GT 86, the new GR 86 gets a horizontally opposed four-cylinder with the choice of either a 6-speed manual or automatic. The engine in the new car has been punched out to 2.4 liters and now makes 228 hp and 184 lb-ft of torque. While that might not sound like much, this little thing only weighs 2,800 pounds and should hit 60 mph in less than 6 seconds. It's also quite practical with a roomy trunk, extra cargo room with the back seats folded, and it gets decent gas mileage too. So this little Toyota will not only help you get your groove back, but it's also going to be a lot of fun to drive back and forth to work. Win-win.

Option C: Bruce Wayne Got Divorced

2022 Audi RS6 Avant
Starting price: $109,000

The divorce finally went through, and she got the house, partial custody of your spoiled children, and an exorbitant amount of your money. You got your freedom and a badass condo. But Buffy and Brett don't fit in the back of your Porsche anymore. So what do you do? Well, you go down to your local Audi purveyor and order up one of these: the 2022 Audi RS6 Avant.

This bitchin' wagon looks like it eats children and small animals as a snack, then feasts on the souls of balding Corvette drivers. Beneath the sinister bodywork is a volcanic 4.0L twin-turbo V8, paired to a 48V mild hybrid system, which sends 591 horsepower & 590 lb-ft of torque to all four wheels via the legendary Audi Quattro AWD system. If you are late to that blind date your sister set up, simply mat the angry pedal, and your family wagon will rocket to 60 mph in an astonishing 3.5 seconds. If the blind date turns out to be crazier than your ex-wife, the Audi facilitates a quick getaway with a top speed of 190 mph (the standard top speed is 174 mph unless you opt for the pricy ceramic brake option).

Blistering performance aside, the 2022 Audi RS6 Avant also has a truly decadent interior made with some of the finest materials in the business. There's also loads of tech and plenty of room for four adults (5 in a pinch). In the cargo area, you have as much space as you would get in a midsize SUV. Which is perfect for hauling Buffy and Bretts' crap around. Or you could fold the rear seats flat for an impromptu romantic tryst with your secretary. Oh, and there are even little hooks molded into the sides of the cargo area, which are ideal for hanging grocery bags or her bra and panties...

If you can't get laid driving this shaggin' wagon, you should probably beg your ex to take you back...

LAURIE YOUNG

"ALL GROWN UP"

Interview by Ron Kuchler
Photos by Mario Barberio
Hair and Makeup by Liz Carrillo

In the pop culture lexicon of iconic moments, there are several which stand out. Bo Derek in 10 in her gold, one-piece swimsuit with braided hair. Raquel Welch in One Million Years B.C. in her neanderthal bikini. Jane Fonda in Barbarella in her silver, metallic two-piece outfit. With those iconic film moments in mind, we set out to recreate on our cover a memorable moment from the days of music videos. Model Laurie Young volunteered as our muse. Do you recognize who (band/singer and actress/model) and the moment we recreated on our cover? Drop us your guess at kandy@kandymag.com . The first ten USA correct guesses will receive a poster-sized version of the cover.

Welcome back Laurie. Is my memory correct in saying the last time we did a Kandy photo shoot together you were pregnant or was there a shoot after that?
Lol, the very last one with Ms. Claudia, yes... pregnant... a little.

One for one on my guesses. Off to a good start. How does it feel to be gracing the cover of our 10 Year Anniversary issue?
It's very exciting and such an honor! I love this magazine and 10 years is such an accomplishment.

Thank you. It seems as if it was just yesterday, we were photographing you, along with Sierra Merchant and Alexa Sandberg for our 2012 Holiday issue. And weren't you recently married around then too?
It does seem like yesterday I feel like we're in some kind of time warp. Awww... I loved that shoot! And Sierra and Alexa are great. Alexa and I still keep in touch. I love her! I did get married in 2011. Geez going on 10 years.

Just like Kandy. Going 10 years strong.
Coincidence, I think not! Haha

When we discussed the photo shoot concept, I laid out a specific target. Because you and I pre-date Kandy, from a working standpoint, I offered you a lot of leeway in the styling of the shoot. What was your motivation behind styling your own shoot?
I wanted this shoot to embody a little more of my personality and where I'm from. Living by the beach my whole life, I thought a beachy chic and surf styled shoot would be the perfect fit. I am very detail oriented, so I tried to style everything, down to the rings. One set was a little more glam than surfer girl, but I really loved both looks.

You nailed your desired look. Plus, you got to work with Mario Barberio again. There seemed to be a lot of synergy between you two on the shoot. Accurate?
Oh yeah! I love Mario! He knows how to make women look beautiful and feel comfortable on top of it. I have loved all the photographers I've

worked with at Kandy, but I do think Mario is my fav.

I believe the shoot was a record for most photos captured. We took 1800 pics. Did you feel like you posed for 1,800 photos?
Not at all!! That's insane how many photos you can take. That just shows how much fun we were having. Well, I was. I can't speak for Mario... haha! Plus, once I get going with looks and jewelry, I just want to keep styling. I really love that side of it.

I can vouch for Mario and say he was having fun. He even said so when the shoot was over. And, as you are aware, I had fun post-shoot posting on my social media the pictures Mario took of me off in the distance.
Aww, he's so sweet.

"I THOUGHT A BEACHY CHIC AND SURF STYLED SHOOT WOULD BE THE PERFECT FIT.

I do not recall Mario ever thanking me for a fun shoot. I am usually the one thanking him. For me, the fun part was watching our crew member spray you down with a garden hose for a half-hour straight. HAHAHA
Those are some great shots. I must admit you had great vision with that concept.

I have my moments.
Lol, that was fun... until it got cold.

Cold? It is southern California and the middle of August.
I'm a wuss with the cold. You should remember that from our NHRA track days.

It is funny you would bring up the NHRA days. As I recall, as we were shooting that last set, I commented to you that this was payback for all the grief you gave me back then.
Yes, yes... you did, and it comes full circle!

It was worth it. We got some amazing photos out of it. Or are you supposed to say that?
They looked so cool straight out of the camera!

We'll come back to those particular photos in a minute. First, let's talk about the different looks. What was the idea with the gold?
I started to look at some old SI swim favorites and also old famous shots of Marisa Miller and other OG supermodels for inspiration. The supermodels of the 90's and early 2000's are my absolute favs. I found a lot of photos styled with some sort of metal top or oversized necklace as a top and I just loved the idea. So, then I found this gorgeous gold number and thought it was perfect.

You made it happen. At first, I wasn't excited about the choice of the orange bikini. I mean, it is an orange bikini, but did you ever put sizzle into that orange. Like this photo for example...
Ahh, I love it! The orange was honestly... because when we initially spoke about styling, I wanted a lack of color, boho theme, but you wanted some pops of color and I saw this and I thought... ooh orange! And gosh... those earrings really pop.

We did have a difference at first. But I finally got my way :)
You always do, but it was a great compromise, and the orange was such a great color out there on the beach.

As you were so involved in the styling of the shoot, it was appropriate for your input on the photos. Share with our readers your initial input.
Wow! Zero editing and I still got it. I guess after having two kids and being locked away because of the state of the world the last 2 years, I didn't know if I'd ever model again. And I certainly didn't feel hot anymore in my sweats and mask. But this gave me the confidence to realize I can keep doing this job that I love so much. It's really been a self-esteem boost seeing these photos!

That certainly was the reaction I was hoping you would share, but as you were leaving me comments on the photos all I kept reading was... cute, these are cute, super cute...
Bahahahahaha... I think cute is the best compliment, but I get it... a kitty or grandpa can be cute.

And I was like Laurie, I'm not looking for cute. Our readers don't want cute. I'm looking for hot, sexy.
I bet the readers don't mind a couple cute shots... ya know... girl next door? Or is that passé?

They can find cute in the Kandy magazine app if they are a subscriber on the app screen titled "FOR YOU". And, of course, as everyone can see, you are hot, sexy.
Aw thanks Ron! I feel hot looking at the pics, especially these orange ones.

In the meantime, our readers deserve a little rawr.
Perfect! Haha

One last comment on the shoot. For the longest time, I have been asking our production teams to put together shoots that pay homage to famous pop culture moments. And this brings us back to soaking you with a garden hose. Will anyone guess the pop culture moment in the red bikini photo where water is flying around you and dripping off your face, hair and body?
I think it's a much hotter version, but someone will guess. I think it's pretty iconic.

I hope so. You weren't exactly on board with the idea. Why don't you tell us whose iconic moment you wanted to recreate?
Raquel Welch, as a cave woman, in One Million Years BC. I thought that was so hot. I heard the movie was terrible, but that's neither here nor there... And I thought you guys should do the Pamela Anderson one with a band on her butt... but a different model.
Those were the two you suggested. Raquel is hot in that film. And we practically did the band one, but we could not align schedules with the intended band.

Shifting gears, besides making babies, what has been keeping you busy?
I have been working on a little side business where I set up boho, luxe styled picnics and parties. It's pretty fun and I have the cutest beach umbrellas and cabanas for our own beach days. I try to work out every day... to keep in shape and I just started surfing again, after a little hiatus.

"I THINK IT'S A MUCH HOTTER VERSION, BUT SOMEONE WILL GUESS. I THINK IT'S PRETTY ICONIC.

Is there a page or Instagram handle people for your side business? **@saltybeachcollective is Instagram**

Don't forget about your part, part, part, part-time gig as my co-host on the Official Kandy Podcast.
Oh yes! I'm the co-host on the Official Kandy Podcast, listen wherever you listen to podcasts.

How is your Kandy trivia these days?
Not great as always. Haha

When you don't know the answer, who inevitably is the answer?
Nikki Leigh! Lol and what's odd is Twitter must be listening because they keep showing me her tweets in my email.

You say Nikki Leigh, you always say Nikki Leigh, but the answer is always Niki Ghazian!
I mean... it's close, am I right? Hahaha

I don't think the ladies would appreciate being called someone else LOL... it's amazing we've yet to have either on the podcast. But we have had enjoyed a few Kandy girls as guests on the show. I probably don't need to ask, but who has been your favorite guest so far?
Obviously, Angie!! But Alexa is a close second.

That would be Angie Smith, NHRA Pro Stock Motorcycle racer. When Alexa was our guest, I could barely manage a word in. I just sat back and let you two run the show. Then, when Katie Lohmann came on our show as a guest, you couldn't arrange a word in. Katie and I go back almost as far as you and I. How difficult is it not to be the center of attention in an industry where you are the center of attention?
Hahaha, yes Katie has a lot to say, but she has great **stories! I think when I first started in this industry, I was young and felt insecure if I wasn't the star of the show, but now I understand every shot needs a certain look and every moment isn't mine. =)**

Well, that is a very adult answer and a long cry from "It's All About the Benjamins Baby!" Sorry readers, inside joke.
I'm such a grown up now :)

You can follow Laurie online on Instagram @dubyoung and see more of these amazing photos in the Kandy magazine app available in the Apple and Amazon appstores.

MISS KANDY SEPTEMBER

ERIN MARIE

Rapid Fire Questions

Dream Destination: Paris, France

Best Feature on a Guy: smile

Personal Feature You Receive the Most Compliments On… Eyes

How Does a Guy Get Your Attention … being a gentleman

How Does a Guy Lose Your Attention … bad hygiene

Open your purse and list the first 3 things you see… Chapstick, sunglasses, pocketknife
Now, the same for the backseat of your car, what do you see… first aid kit

If you could meet any person, alive or dead, who would it be? Walt Disney, Jim Henson, and Robin Williams (such creative minds to learn from)

First modeling job? swimwear boutique catalog shoot

Where do you see yourself in 5 years? working full-time in TV/film

Dream profession? currently pursuing a more full-time tv/film career

Describe your Kandy Magazine photoshoot experience. So much fun working with photographer Mike Prado! He is professional, kind, and super talented!

KANDYGRAM

SHAE
HOMETOWN: DALLAS, TEXAS
PHOTOGRAPHER MIKE PRADO

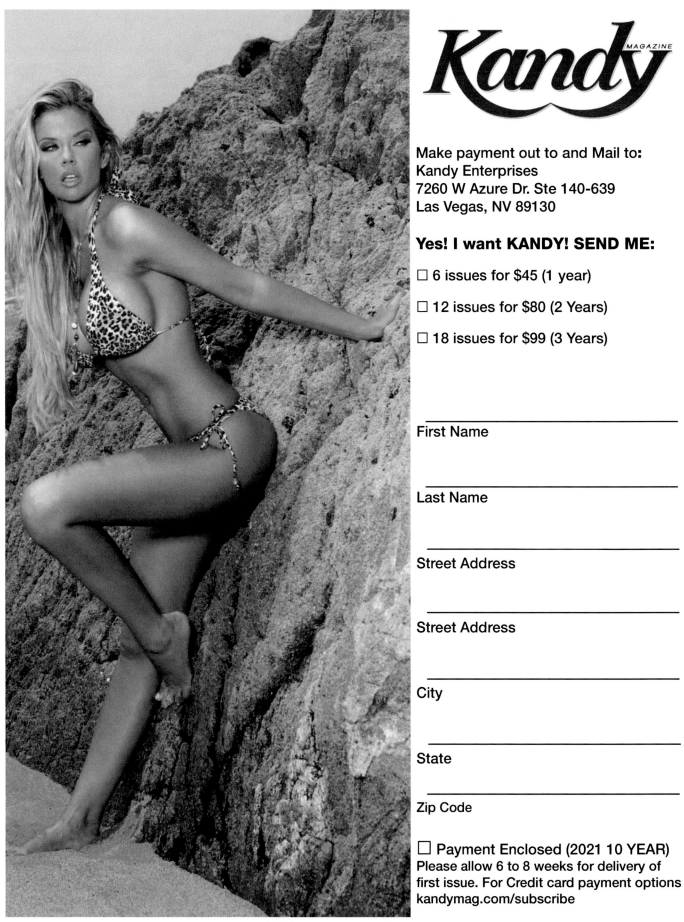

Make payment out to and Mail to:
Kandy Enterprises
7260 W Azure Dr. Ste 140-639
Las Vegas, NV 89130

Yes! I want KANDY! SEND ME:

☐ 6 issues for $45 (1 year)

☐ 12 issues for $80 (2 Years)

☐ 18 issues for $99 (3 Years)

_____
First Name

_____
Last Name

_____
Street Address

_____
Street Address

_____
City

_____
State

_____
Zip Code

☐ Payment Enclosed (2021 10 YEAR)
Please allow 6 to 8 weeks for delivery of
first issue. For Credit card payment options
kandymag.com/subscribe

Madden 22

Platforms: PlayStation®5, Xbox® Series X|S, PC via Origin™, Steam, Xbox One, PlayStation 4, Stadia
Developer: EA Tiburon
Rating: E
Kandy Rating: BUY, BUY, BUY

Kandy Says

We took a long hiatus from video games, rightfully so. However, with Madden 22 our enthusiasm for the pop culture niche has returned. Just when we thought we were out, Madden 22 has brought us back in. What is it about Madden 22 that has us all fired up? Dynamic Gameday! This feature is made for football. Gameday atmosphere? Come on! How amazing to have the 12th Man in your corner? The frozen tundra of Green Bay? Hold onto that frozen rock. Sorry babes. We've discovered Madden 22. Our night out will need to be pushed to January.

Synopsis

Best New Feature - New Dynamic Gameday
What it does? impacts gameplay across every mode. Whether you are installing a weekly gameplan in Franchise or going head-to-head in Play Now, games will feel fresh with a deeper level of strategy and storytelling in each match-up and in each stadium

Dynamic Gameday is powered by three new features:

- Gameday Atmosphere - connects you to NFL fandom through the crowds, environments, and presentation elements that enhance and impact every game
- Gameday Momentum - performance-based mechanics, including Home Field Advantage* which provides a unique game condition tailored to each NFL team's stadium atmosphere, swing momentum, bringing the tangible influence of momentum to life on the field
- Next Gen Stats: Star-Driven AI - powered by real world player data that will evolve throughout the season, changes AI behavior and team tendencies to make NFL superstars and the personality of each team more true-to-life

Returning Features and Upgrades

Franchise Mode makes you feel more connected and in control of your team, with more detailed staff management and skill tree progression systems, and comprehensive weekly game strategy with a revamped Season Engine that keeps things fresh every week. Franchise will continue to see improvements throughout the year via multiple live service updates.

Madden NFL's newest mode, The Yard, features an all-new single player campaign and avatar progression system that shares progress, rewards and vanity with Face of the Franchise.

Face of The Franchise returns with an all-new story, player class system, and the option to play on the defensive side of the ball as a linebacker for the first time.

Superstar KO brings multiplayer squad play to NFL teams with the addition of real-world NFL teams to the mode for the first time.

Madden Ultimate Team offers a new season of content, allows for halftime adjustments to Superstar X-Factors and integrates Next Gen Stats* to track stats for player items.

THE Many Saints OF Newark

Rated: R
Genre: Drama
Starring: Alessandro Nivola, Leslie Odom Jr., Jon Bernthal, Corey Stoll, Michael Gandolfini, Billy Magnussen, Michela De Rossi, John Magaro, Ray Liotta, Vera Farmiga
Director: Alan Taylor
Studio: New Line Cinema
PHOTOGRAPHS Barry Wetcher

Synopsis
"The Many Saints of Newark" is the much-anticipated feature film prequel to the HBO drama series "The Sopranos." The film is set in the explosive era of the Newark riots, when rival gangsters began to rise up, challenging the all-powerful DiMeo crime family's hold over the city.

Young Anthony Soprano is growing up in one of the most tumultuous eras in Newark's history, becoming a man just as rival gangsters begin to rise up and challenge the all-powerful DiMeo crime family's hold over the increasingly race-torn city. Caught up in the changing times is the uncle he idolizes, Dickie Moltisanti, who struggles to manage both his professional and personal responsibilities—and whose influence over his nephew will help make the impressionable teenager into the all-powerful mob boss we'll later come to know: Tony Soprano.

> ### "Some babies when they come into the world, know all sorts of things from the other side"

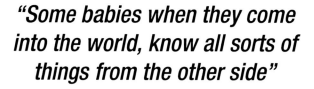

Kandy Says
The line which closes at end of the trailer to "The Many Saints of Newark". Baby Christopher cries as he is introduced to a young Tony Soprano at the dinner table. A perfect foreshadowing of the bind the two will have later in life. Fans of the show will like the movie. Fans of mafia films will leave disappointed. The fan is not in the same class as any of the Godfather films, including Godfather 3. It falls far short of Casino, Goodfellas... fill in the blank of your favorite mafia film.

Women of America
Missouri

BRI STERN
PHOTOGRAPHER MIKE PRADO
HOMETOWN ST. LOUIS, MO
LOCATION: LOS ANGELES, CA

MADE IN
U.S.A.

MADE IN
U.S.A.

2021 NATIONAL FOOTBALL LEAGUE PREVIEW

With the 2021 NFL season upon us, two certainties are crystal clear, unless a slew of catastrophic injuries befalls the Tampa Bay Buccaneers, TB12 will lead the Bucs to consecutive Super Bowl titles, and the toughest division in football is the NFC West. However, we were also confident that the NL East in MLB was the best division in baseball. We were all very wrong. However, in our opinion, any one of the four NFC West teams could win the division. They all are that good. For our money, we are picking the Los Angeles Rams, as we believe the addition of Matt Stafford completes the puzzle on the offensive side of the ball. Agree or disagree with our choices and reasoning? Let us know and #talktokandy by sending us an email to editor@kandymag.com. We'll publish our reader's responses in the next issue of Kandy.

American Football Conference

Who will face the Bucs in next year's Super Bowl in Los Angeles? Vegas bookies say the Chiefs in a rematch of the game played earlier this year. Do they realize how difficult it is to appear in three straight Super Bowls these days? Unless it is the New England Patriots and Tom Brady is under center, it is nearly impossible. We say one of the wild-card teams emerge from the pact and make it to LA to take on the Bucs.

East

The Bills are the sexy experts pick to dethrone the Chiefs as AFC champs. We're not confident they even win the AFC East. We definitely don't have the balls to say it aloud, nor make the prediction, but don't be surprised if the Miami Dolphins not only win the division but advance to the Super Bowl. Buffalo Bills
Miami Dolphins
New England Patriots
New York Jets

North

The second toughest division in football? Hard to argue against it, but that all depends on how well the Steelers compete this year. Do the Browns have enough depth to advance to the AFC Championship game? Maybe.

Cleveland Browns
Pittsburgh Steelers
Baltimore Ravens
Cincinnati Bengals

South

Titans? Colts? Titans? Who will it be? We'll pick the Titans to pound their way into the playoffs.

Tennessee Titans
Indianapolis Colts
Houston Texans
Jacksonville Jaguars

West

Is this the most overlooked division in football? How good are the three teams behind the Chiefs? Can the Chargers stay healthy? How much will they miss TE Hunter Henry? Is Teddy Bridgewater the quarterback the Broncos have been seeking since Peyton Manning retired? Is there Black Magic in the Vegas desert?

Kansas City Chiefs
Los Angeles Chargers
Las Vegas Raiders
Denver Broncos

National Football Conference

The Panthers surprise everyone and claim a wild-card spot. The Cowboys reclaim the NFC East crown. With all four teams mathematically in contention for the division title, the NFC West does not crown a champion until the final week of the season.

East

A healthy Zak Prescott equals a Cowboys NFC East title. The Eagles and Giants battle for second place, neither with a realistic playoff chance. The No-name team in Washington has a stout defense that eventually is worn out by a no-gain offense.

Dallas Cowboys
Philadelphia Eagles
New York Giants
Washington No-names

South

Tom Brady leads the Bucs to a repeat division crown and consecutive Super Bowl titles. Sam Darnold leads his new team, the Carolina Panthers, to a wild-card playoff game. Jameis Winston is solid in replacing Drew Brees in New Orleans, and the Atlanta Falcons rebuild is evident.

Tampa Bay Buccaneers
Carolina Panthers
New Orleans Saints
Atlanta Falcons

North

The Packers win the division. The Bears surprise the league and wind up second. The Vikings and Lions continue to disappoint fans.

Green Bay Packers
Chicago Bears
Minnesota Vikings
Detroit Lions

West (The Best Division in the NFL)

Matthew Stafford. Russell Wilson. Jimmy Garoppolo. Kyler Murray. The NFC West is our pick for the division with the best Qb's, top to bottom. We're not going to rank them.

Los Angeles Rams
San Francisco 49ers
Arizona Cardinals
Seattle Seahawks

Make checks out to and Mail to:
KANDY
7260 W. Azure Dr. Ste 140-639
Las Vegas, NV 89130

Yes! I want KANDY! SEND ME:

☐ **6 issues for $45 (1 Year*)**
INDIVIDUAL Print Cover Price $71.94

☐ **12 issues for $80 (2 Years*)**
INDIVIDUAL Print Cover Price $143.88

_____

First Name

_____

Last Name

_____

Street Address

_____

Street Address

_____

City

_____

State

_____

Zip Code

☐ Payment Enclosed
Please allow 8 to 10weeks for delivery of first
issue.

* 6 Print issues per year
For Credit card and other payment options
kandymag.com/subscribe
2021 10 YEAR ANNIVERSARY

Made in the USA
Las Vegas, NV
15 December 2023

82882014R00026